Bluebird Rescue

Bluebird Rescue

by Joan Rattner Heilman

illustrated with full-color photographs

Lothrop, Lee & Shepard Books
New York

The author would like to thank the North American Bluebird Society for its invaluable help in the research for this book.

Photographs on pages 2, 6, 11 (top), 18, 19, 26, 30, 34, 42–43 by Michael L. Smith; page 11 (bottom) by Ted Oberman; page 15 (top) by Hubert W. Prescott; pages 15 (bottom), 38, 39 (left) by Lorne Scott; page 23 courtesy North American Bluebird Society; page 39 (right) by Fred Lahrman; pages 47–48 by Lawrence Zeleny.

1 2 3 4 5 6 7 8 9 10

Library of Congress Cataloging in Publication Data
Heilman, Joan Rattner.   Bluebird rescue.
Summary: Explains the nesting, feeding, and breeding habits of bluebirds and instructs how to protect this endangered species.   1. Bluebirds—Juvenile literature.   2. Birds, Protection of—Juvenile literature.   3. Birds, Attracting of—Juvenile Literature. [1. Bluebirds.   2. Birds—Protection.   3. Birds—Attracting.   4. Wildlife conservation]   I. Title.
QL696.P288H44   639.9′78842   81-17191
ISBN 0-688-00894-1   AACR2   ISBN 0-688-00895-X (lib. bdg.)

Contents

This male Eastern Bluebird makes it easy to see why bluebirds were called "blue robins" by America's early settlers.

Where Have All the Bluebirds Gone?

If you have ever seen a bluebird, you are really lucky. Most people haven't, even though not very many years ago these shy little thrushes flashed around almost everybody's backyard. When your grandparents were young, bluebirds were almost as common as robins are today, but so beautiful that they were America's favorite bird from the time of the first settlers.

With their radiant blue feathers, soft round bodies, appealing little faces, and gentle manner, bluebirds came to symbolize hope, happiness, springtime, and love. More songs were written about them than any other bird in our history, and one famous writer, Henry David Thoreau, said that bluebirds carry the sky on their backs.

In some parts of North America, the only place in the world (except Bermuda) where bluebirds are found, you can still find them raising broods of babies in the spring and summer. Or perhaps you'll see a few dozen of them flying south on sunny days in the fall, once known as "bluebird weather." But bluebirds are vanishing from the earth and, if they don't get some help from us, they may soon become extinct, just as many other birds and animals already have.

There are three species of bluebirds. In the greatest danger are Eastern Bluebirds (scientific name: *Sialia sialis*), the little blue-backed, rosy-breasted birds that you see so often on greeting cards. Scientists estimate that there is now only one Eastern Bluebird for every ten that lived only forty years ago. The numbers of Mountain (*Sialia currucoides*) and Western (*Sialia mexicana*) Bluebirds, the other two species, are getting smaller, too, though not as quickly.

The bluebirds' biggest problem is a serious housing shortage. Their habitat is disappearing under layers of concrete and asphalt. Houses, highways, shopping centers, parking lots, industries, huge commercial farms, and railroads have taken over much of the land that once was home to bluebirds and many other native birds like woodpeckers, nuthatches, and great blue herons.

In addition, bluebirds are extremely fussy about where they make their nests. They won't nest in cities or crowded suburbs and they hate forests or deep shade. Instead, they insist on open spaces, with not too many trees or buildings around them. They will nest only in small enclosures or holes, and they have always loved rotten wooden fence posts, dark hollows in decaying trees, knotholes, and abandoned woodpecker holes. Unfortunately, today most fences are made of metal, dead tree limbs are often zapped by chain saws, and there aren't as many open fields and meadows around as there were even twenty years ago.

Of course, not every natural nesting hole is gone. But the remaining possibilities are usually taken over by a couple of other birds, immigrants from Europe. These two tough birds, starlings and house sparrows (often called English sparrows), were imported from England during the last century and, because they found few natural enemies here, they soon became the most common birds in many parts of the continent. House sparrows arrived in America by invitation from well-meaning bird lovers in the 1850s. Starlings came in 1880 when eighty of them were released in New York's Central Park. They loved it there. They loved it everywhere they went.

Unfortunately for bluebirds, starlings and sparrows also like to build their nests in holes, though they will settle for other places. They are much more aggressive than the gentle bluebirds and when there is competition for a hole, they almost always win. If bluebirds or other native birds happen to move into a hole first, starlings and sparrows often break their eggs or kill the babies, and sometimes even the adult bluebirds as well. Then they may take over the nesting holes themselves.

When starlings and sparrows take over the holes of some other hardy, cavity-nesting birds, like woodpeckers and chickadees, those birds will flee into the woods to find another place to nest. But bluebirds are not so adaptable. They must have open spaces or they won't nest at all.

Food is another problem. Bluebirds are ground feeders and live mostly on insects. Chemical pesticides used in recent years to kill crop-damaging insects may be good for some crops, but they are not good for birds. They kill the insects bluebirds need for food and they may even kill some birds as well.

In late summer and fall and in early spring and winter, bluebirds also eat berries. Starlings are very fond of berries, too, and turn out in huge flocks to feast on them. Most of the time, they strip the trees and bushes almost bare so there is very little left for less aggressive birds to eat.

For a while after they came to this continent, starlings and sparrows made life very difficult only for Eastern Bluebirds. But now those two European birds have gone west, affecting the populations of Mountain and Western Bluebirds as well.

Not all of the bluebirds' troubles come from other birds and people. They have natural enemies, too, including bitter cold weather. In recent winters—especially the winters of 1977 and 1978—the normally warm areas of North America have been struck by severe cold spells. Each time, many bluebirds have died, either from freezing or starvation, especially when their food supply has been buried under snow and ice. And, of course, bluebirds have to watch out for cats and raccoons, squirrels

House sparrows (top) and starlings (bottom) compete with bluebirds for nesting holes and food—with bluebirds usually losing the fight.

and snakes, as well as dangerous two-footed human animals.

All in all, life has become extremely difficult. There is very little that concerned citizens can do to save many of our birds and animals from extinction, except to contribute money to wildlife organizations or to urge their representatives in Congress to pass laws that protect them. But bluebirds are different. Their future depends on the efforts of individuals like you.

What can you do? You can build bluebird houses, put them up in the right places, and watch over them during the nesting season. When bluebirds move in, you can protect them from their enemies. You can plant bushes or trees or vines with the kinds of berries bluebirds like to eat. And you can ask others to stop using pesticides that kill the birds and the insects they eat. If you think these seem like small steps, you're wrong. For bluebirds to increase in number, they *must* have proper housing—it's the only way they can survive.

The North American Bluebird Society was started in 1978 to encourage people to put up bluebird houses, to gather information about the birds, and to research even better ways to protect them. Dr. Lawrence Zeleny, its founder, says, "Bluebirds are well on their way to complete dependence on our help if they are going to survive. With enough effort from us, they can make it. It's up to *us* whether America's favorite bird will live or become only a memory like the passenger pigeon."

Watching Bluebirds Grow

Bluebirds belong to the thrush family, which also includes robins and veerys. All thrushes are good singers and have young with spotted breasts.

The Eastern Bluebird is only a little larger than a sparrow, about five and a half inches long. It has a carpet of rich blue feathers on its head, back, and tail, earthy red feathers on its round breast, and a soft white belly. This species is found from the Atlantic coast west to the Rocky Mountains, from southern Canada to the Gulf of Mexico and to the mountains of central Mexico.

The Western Bluebird looks very much like the Eastern Bluebird, but it has a blue throat and the red on its breast extends across its shoulders. It makes its home along the West Coast, from Canada into Mexico.

The Mountain Bluebird breeds in the West and across the Rocky Mountains, living mainly in meadows and clearings in high altitudes below the timberline. This species is slimmer and slightly longer than the other two—about six inches from beak to tail—and has no red feathers. It is all bright turquoise blue except for its pale blue belly.

Like many other birds, female bluebirds are much less colorful than the males. Often they look more gray than blue except for the ends of their wings and tails. Young birds, both male and female, are mottled gray with telltale blue around the edges of their wings and tails. Their breasts are speckled, and they look similar to immature robins. In the fall, they molt their baby feathers and by the winter they look like adult birds.

Bluebirds are shy birds who rarely raise their voices and usually fight only when they are defending their nests, often losing the battle. They don't sing very loudly and they will never win any awards for their tunes, though many people find nothing more pleasing than their soft, gentle warbling. Someone once said they were saying, "Dear, dear! Think of it, think of it!"

The Mountain and Western species do most of their warbling so early in the morning that they aren't heard very often by human ears. Eastern Bluebirds sound off more frequently as they sit on a branch or a fence, hunched over in their round-shouldered way. All bluebirds do their best singing during the short courting season in early spring, when they really go overboard with enthusiasm.

At the first hint of spring, the male bluebird gets busy. He starts hunting for the right hole for a nest. When he

The coloration differences among the three bluebird species are more marked in the male. Compare the Western Bluebird (top) and the Mountain Bluebird (bottom) to the Eastern Bluebird on page 6.

finds one, he invites his mate to take a look at it. She is the one who will decide if it is suitable for raising a brood. While she sits on a nearby branch or wire, her fine-feathered mate flies in and out of the hole he has selected and sings just as loudly and beautifully as he can. He flutters his bright blue wings and spreads his blue tail, and brings the female an insect or two to show what a good father he will be. When she finally consents to enter the hole for an inspection tour, he encourages her with even more songs.

The female bluebird makes the nest, building the home out of soft dry grasses or fragrant pine needles. Then she lays small blue eggs, though once in a while her eggs are pure white. She lays three or four, or even seven or eight, and sits on them to incubate them until they hatch about two weeks later. Meanwhile, the male's job is to guard their home, keep on singing, and bring her a delicious grasshopper or caterpillar now and then. If an enemy comes near, the father will chatter and swoop, and some-times even attack quite fiercely.

Bluebirds also insist upon their territorial rights. This means that they "stake out" a certain area for themselves and will not allow another bluebird family to live too close by, though other kinds of birds don't bother them as much. Often they will live happily right next door to tree swallows or chickadees or other native birds.

Baby bluebirds, like all little birds, are always very hun-gry, keeping both parents occupied with bringing them food. Each one of them is fed a tasty insect about every twenty minutes from before sunrise until after sunset. If there are five or six nestlings, you can see why their mother and father don't have much time for anything else.

When the babies are ready to leave the nest after about seventeen or eighteen days, their parents let them get a little hungry. Then they lure them out of the nest by dangling an insect just out of reach and warbling an encouraging song. Baby bluebirds know instinctively how to fly. They flap their small wings and usually manage to flutter to a nearby tree or bush. For a few weeks, until they learn how to capture their own food, they are fed by their parents.

Bluebirds often raise two and sometimes three broods of babies every year, so the nesting season may last from February until early August. This keeps everybody busy. The father keeps his eye on the first brood of birds after they leave the nest, making sure they get enough to eat and aren't consumed by cats or raccoons. The mother, meanwhile, gets right to work building a new nest. When a new batch of nestlings is hatched, their older brothers and sisters sometimes help bring them food and the whole family usually stays together in the same neighborhood for the summer.

Bluebirds have a huge appetite for insects, especially those that farmers and gardeners are glad to get rid of, such as cutworms, grasshoppers, crickets, and beetles. They usually catch them by sitting on the limb of a tree, a power line, or a fence post, and then dropping suddenly down to the ground to pounce on their next meal. Mountain Bluebirds like to hover low over the ground in their search for food. When the weather turns cold and insects are scarce, all three species feed mainly on berries.

In warm climates, bluebirds may stay in the same neighborhood all year long. But those that nest in the northern parts of the United States and Canada must

The female bluebird incubates the eggs until they hatch.

migrate before the weather gets too cold. Though years ago bluebirds migrated in large flocks, turning a gray sky blue, today only about fifteen or twenty of them usually make the trip together. These few families will gradually keep moving south in the fall as the temperatures drop. They will return once again to their old habitats in the early spring.

Then she and the male are kept busy feeding the hungry brood.

Building and Mounting a Nesting Box

If you would like to have bluebird families as your neighbors, then you must provide a home for them. It must be made to certain specifications so that bluebirds like it and starlings can't fit into it, and mounted where sparrows won't be too tempted to move in.

The size of the entrance hole is especially important. It must be precisely 1½ inches in diameter—no bigger *or* smaller. If you make it smaller, bluebirds may be unable to get into the house. If you make it even ⅛ inch bigger, starlings may squeeze through. Don't add a perch on the front of the box. Bluebirds don't need one and it gives enemy birds a handy foothold for attacking.

Depth is another important factor. Allow at least 6 inches from the bottom of the entrance hole to the floor so that starlings, cats, raccoons, and other predators will find it difficult to reach the bluebird eggs or baby birds inside.

To keep the box from becoming too hot or too cold, your birdhouse should be constructed from wood at least ¾ inch thick for good insulation. Be sure to cut the corners off the side and bottom boards to make openings for ventilation and drainage.

Finally, the nesting box should be easy for you to open for cleaning and observing. But it shouldn't be so easy to open that other people will be tempted to disturb your tenants.

It's simple to make a nesting box if you follow the plans given in the next chapters. However, if you aren't used to handling tools, you should ask an adult to help you. You can also purchase ready-made nesting boxes from the North American Bluebird Society (write to Box 6295, Silver Spring, Maryland 20905).

For making your own, you can use any kind of wood, though most people use pine because it is the least expensive. Maybe you can find some old pieces of wood in your basement or garage, enough to make a birdhouse or two. Or you can use *exterior* grade plywood unless there are lots of porcupines in your neighborhood—porcupines like to eat plywood.

There is no need to paint the box, though painting will make it last longer, especially if you use pine. Boxes made of cedar, redwood, cypress, or exterior grade plywood need not be painted to make them more durable. If you paint, be sure to choose a *light* color, because it will reflect heat and keep the box cooler. Use exterior latex paint. Or you may finish the outside with natural alkyd wood sealer or spar varnish. But *do not* paint, seal, or varnish the inside of the box or the edges of the entrance hole and *do not* use chemical wood preservatives.

After you have made your nesting box, you must mount it in the right location, at a certain height, and in a special way if you want to attract bluebirds and watch them raise their families. This is extremely important, even more important than the way you build the house, because bluebirds won't settle in unless the house is located in a place they like.

Bluebirds insist on open land for their housing, with no tall grass or weeds. They like sunshine and space, preferably on a high ridge, with a few scattered trees or high shrubs and fences not more than about one hundred feet away in direct view of their front door. This is because fledglings need a safe place to land when they leave the nest for the first time. And adult birds like a high perch so they can spot insects on the ground below.

If you don't live on a farm or out in the country, you may need permission to use somebody else's land for your bluebird house. Remember, it should be mounted close enough to your own home so it can be easily monitored during nesting season. Good sites include golf courses, large cemeteries, nature preserves, fields, big lawns and estates, orchards, farmland, meadows, or the edges of rural roads—all open spaces where chemical poisons are not heavily used.

Bluebirds will nest only in open spaces, like this field.

Moving day for bluebirds comes in the early spring. In southern areas, house hunting begins by the middle of February. In the northern states and Canada, it begins in mid- or late March. So your nesting box should be built and mounted before then. If you have made more than one box, place each at least one hundred yards apart to satisfy the bluebirds' territorial instincts.

Remember, too, not everybody loves birds. Try to locate your box or boxes in places where they won't attract much attention.

You can attach your bluebird house to a wooden or metal pole, or to the trunk of an isolated tree that faces an open area. If you use an existing fence post or utility pole, be sure to get permission from its owners or one day you may find your nesting box has been removed.

The ideal height for a bluebird house is 3 to 5 feet from the ground to the bottom of the box. Though bluebirds are perfectly willing to live in a higher house, there are two reasons to mount it low. One is house sparrows, who don't like to nest so close to the ground. The other is convenience—if the box is low, you will be able to reach it more easily when you want to observe the nest or clean out the house.

If you mount your nesting box on a post in a pasture, place it high enough so the animals can't rub it off. On a fence around a pasture, place it on the outside of the post. If you choose a busy area, such as a golf course or well-used nature preserve, mount your box out of reach —even though it means taking a small lightweight ladder with you when you monitor it.

Heat is something else to keep in mind. If the temperature in your area often goes above 95 degrees Fahrenheit, place the house where it will be somewhat shaded during the hottest part of the day, perhaps on the north or northeast side of a large pole or on the trunk of an isolated tree. But *don't* put it in among the branches of the tree or in the woods. If you don't live in a hot part of the country, you can safely mount the nesting box in a sunny location and face it in any direction you like.

Here's how to attach your house:

• On a wooden post or tree, screw or nail the box in place, using the holes you have drilled in the back board.

• On a metal pole, attach the house with bolts or wire. Or you may choose a ½-inch or ¾-inch galvanized pipe with threads at one end. Attach a pipe flange to the bottom of the box. Plant the unthreaded end of the pipe at least 1½ feet into the ground. Then twist the birdhouse onto the flange at the top.

If you live in an area where house sparrows are a serious problem and always take over your nesting box before bluebirds can move in, then you may want to try putting up "jug houses" made out of empty plastic bleach bottles. Though bluebirds much prefer wooden boxes, they will accept jugs if no other homes are available. On the other hand, house sparrows don't seem to like them at all. Neither do tree swallows, who are very competitive with bluebirds for homes in some parts of the Northeast.

Jug houses are much simpler to make than wooden boxes, and the bottles don't cost you anything. You will need the large one-gallon size with a cap.

The jug must be well insulated with paint, because it holds heat. Always cover it with three coats, using an exterior latex paint. Choose white or yellow or another very pale color that will reflect the heat and keep the inside of the jug cool enough for the birds.

Just like the hole in a wooden nesting box, the entrance hole in a jug house must be exactly 1½ inches in diameter, no more and no less. If you are not allowed to

*If you mount your jug house or nesting box next to a pasture, make
sure it is safe from other animals.*

handle a sharp knife or a power drill with a hole saw, be
sure to ask an adult to cut the hole for you. Directions for
making a jug house are on page 32.

To attach the house to a post, you will need an 8-inch
piece of wire. Curve it slightly and pass it through one of

the two holes you have punched (near the bottom of the jug under the handle) and out the second hole. Hold the jug against the mounting post and wrap the wire around it, twisting the wire tightly with a pair of pliers. Insert a second piece of 8-inch wire through the hole formed by the jug's handle and wrap it around the post, securing it with the pliers as before.

Now, whether you have made a wooden nesting box or a jug house, you are ready to welcome your first guests in the spring.

How to Make a
Bluebird Nesting Box

Materials needed:

Lumber: ¾ inch thick, cut to the dimensions shown in the diagram. Remember to cut off the corners of the bottom board and the top corners of the sides. These will provide openings for ventilation and drainage.

Screw: 1½-inch wood screw with washer

Nails: 1½-inch galvanized siding nails or aluminum nails

Tools: saw, hammer, screwdriver, drill, expansion bit and hand auger

Paint (light color), wood sealer or spar varnish: optional

1. Drill the holes in the back board as shown in the diagram. These will be used to mount the box.
2. Cut the entrance hole carefully—it cannot be even a tiny bit larger than 1½ inches in diameter—with the expansion bit and hand auger. Or, better yet, ask an experienced adult to cut it with a 1½-inch hole saw attached to a power drill.

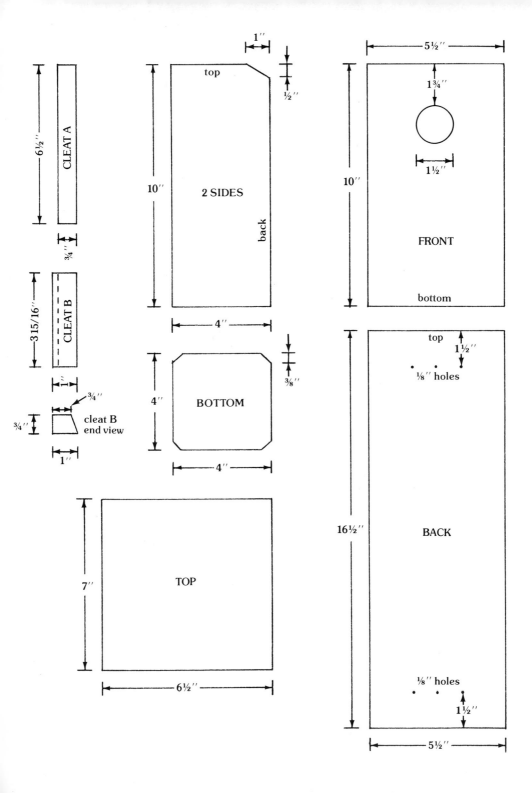

You need not paint your nesting box. This one is slightly deeper than the one you are building and has a slanted instead of flat roof.

3. Place the side boards on the back board two inches from the top, making sure the edges are square. Nail the back board to each side piece, placing the three nails on each side about 3 inches apart.
4. Nail the front to the two sides, again using three nails about 3 inches apart.
5. Hold the top board in place. Nail cleat A to the back board as shown in the diagram so that the cleat is square with the top piece.

6. Still holding the top in place, reach through the bottom of the box and place cleat B in the correct position. Remove the top and cleat B, holding them together securely. Move the cleat about $\frac{1}{16}$ inch toward the back board edge and then nail it in place.
7. Slide the bottom board about ¼ inch into the box as shown in the side view diagram. Nail it securely around all four sides.
8. With the top board in position, drill a $\frac{3}{16}$-inch hole for a screw through that board to about ½ inch into the upper edge of the front board (see side view).
9. Secure the top board with the screw and washer.

For finishing and mounting instructions, see pages 21–22, 24–25.

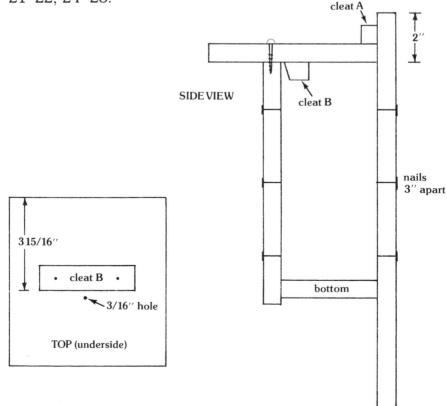

How to Make a
Bluebird Jug House

Materials needed:

Jug: one-gallon plastic bleach bottle with cap

Paint: exterior latex in a light color

Wire: 2 8-inch pieces (for attaching to post)

Tools: sharp knife or power drill with hole saw attachment, rounded wood file or piece of sandpaper, screwdriver or large nail.

1. Wash the jug thoroughly, rinsing it many times.
2. Cover the jug with three coats of paint.
3. Cut the entrance hole, using the knife or power drill. You may have to ask an adult for help with this. Make the hole precisely 1½ inches in diameter. The bottom of the hole should be about 6 inches from the base of the bottle on the opposite side from the handle.
4. Smooth the edges of the entrance hole with the file or sandpaper.
5. Using the screwdriver or nail, punch four or five drainage holes in the bottom of the jug. Also punch a hole just below the jug handle for ventilation and two holes on the handle side about 2 inches apart and about 1 inch from the jug bottom.

For mounting instructions, see page 26.

Monitoring the Birdhouse

After you have built and mounted your bluebird house, you will need to wait patiently for the birds to move in. If you're very lucky, they will choose your house right away. If you're not quite so lucky, they may come the next year. Getting the first pair of birds to settle in your house is the hardest. Once they make a home there, however, your bluebird population will probably grow larger every year if you build more houses for them.

Meanwhile, you have several important jobs to do. During the nesting season, you must inspect the birdhouse at least once a week. Every day is even better. You will need to remove the nest of any house sparrows who've decided you've made the house just for them. You don't have to be concerned about starlings settling in if you have made the entrance hole the right size.

Don't feel sorry for the sparrows you throw out—they won't be homeless for long. They don't require special birdhouses or even holes for their nests. Like starlings, they will happily nest almost anywhere. Even if you evict the sparrows after they have laid some eggs, they will just build a new nest and lay new eggs.

You will learn to recognize a sparrow's straw and weed

33

nest, which is usually lined with feathers and trash such as paper, plastic, and pieces of cloth. It is bulky, deep, and often domed at the top, with an entrance on the side. Sparrows' eggs are gray-white with gray or brown speckles.

Bluebirds' nests are made almost entirely of dry grasses or pine needles, and are quite neatly arranged. The best way to find out whose nest is in your birdhouse is to sit quietly a safe distance away and watch to see what kinds of birds go in.

Sparrows are very stubborn. They may return again and again to the bluebird house, starting new nests. But you must be stubborn, too. Remove them—every day if necessary. They will always find somewhere else to live. To remove a nest from a nesting box is quite simple. All you have to do is reach in and take it out. For a jug house, the task is a little harder. Take a wire coat hanger and open it up into a long piece of wire hooked at one end. Then, unscrew the jug's cap, push the wire into the jug, and pull out the nest with the hook. If you prefer, you may take the jug off its post, take it home with you, and remove the nest by hosing it out before you hang it up again.

Don't other birds use bluebird houses? Yes, they do. And many of them are just as nice to have around as

Bluebirds' clear blue (sometimes pure white) eggs are never speckled like sparrows'.

bluebirds, though they may not be as beautiful. If other native hole-nesting birds, such as chickadees, titmice, tree swallows, or nuthatches, move into your house, don't send them packing. Let them stay, put up some more nesting boxes, and hope for bluebirds the next time around.

Your last job of the year is an easy one, but it is very important, too. In the fall or winter, give your nesting box a final inspection. Take out any old nests, wash the box if a hose is handy, make any necessary repairs, and be sure the drainage holes are open.

Your birdhouse is now all ready for occupancy when the bluebirds return once again.

Bluebird Care and Feeding

In the winter and early spring, when insects are scarce and bluebirds turn to berries, you may be able to lure the birds to your nesting box with food if they remain in your part of the country all year. (They will enjoy a bird bath, too.) Most berries, such as strawberries and blueberries, don't last until winter. But there are some that get hard and tough and do not drop off no matter how strong the wind blows or how low the temperature drops. Although these berries may not look very good to us, the birds are happy to eat them when they are hungry.

Some berry plants, like sumac, are wild. Others must be purchased at a nursery. Be sure to find out how to plant them correctly.

On the next page are some of the most common plants whose berries appeal to bluebirds and many other desirable birds. Some of them have berries that last well into the winter. Of course, not every berry tree, shrub, or vine will grow everywhere, so it is important to find out which ones will survive in your climate:

American holly	Mistletoe
Bayberry (wax myrtle)	Mountain ash
Bittersweet	Mulberry
Black alder	Multiflora rose
Black cherry	Pin cherry
Common chokeberry	Pyracantha (firethorn)
Dogwood	Red cedar
Elderberry	Shadberry (serviceberry)
Hackberry	Sumac
Hawthorn	Virginia creeper
Honeysuckle	Wild grape

Be careful not to disturb the eggs or the babies.

Though bluebirds don't eat seeds and so aren't interested in the usual kinds of outdoor bird food, you can fill a feeder with other food they *do* like: raisins and other dried fruits, chopped unsalted nuts, suet, finely cracked corn or cornmeal, or peanut hearts. If there are bluebirds in your neighborhood in the winter or early spring, you may find them eating at your feeder.

When bluebirds are living in your birdhouse, try not to bother them too much. You can easily frighten them away, especially while they are building their nest. Until the nest is completed and the eggs are laid, observe only from a distance. After that, they won't mind too much if you open the top of the box and take a very fast look

here Mountain Bluebirds, in your nesting box.

once in a while just to see what is going on. Then close the box again very quickly. To check on the occupants of a jug house, just look into the entrance hole.

Never, never touch the nest or the eggs or the baby birds. (Exception: If there are dead birds, remove them with a paper towel or a pair of tongs and bury them. Of course, it's always a good idea to wash your hands afterward.) Before you open the box, tap the side lightly to warn the mother you are there and give her a chance to fly away.

Cats, raccoons, opossums, snakes, squirrels, and skunks all consider birds or eggs to be tasty snacks. They will climb up poles and trees and reach inside nests for food. You have already helped protect your bluebird family from its enemies by making your nesting box the right depth with the entrance hole in the right place. But if there are many climbing animals in your area, you can protect the birds in other ways. You can, for example, mount the house on a thin metal pole and then keep the pole very slippery. Spread soft automobile grease on the pole every week or so during the nesting season. The grease must be fresh, because if it hardens up, it may make the pole even easier for an animal to climb.

You can also make a "raccoon guard" to attach to the entrance hole of the birdhouse. Take a board 1½ or 2 inches thick and about 3 inches square. Cut a hole in it exactly 1½ inches in diameter to match the entrance hole. Nail or screw it to the front of the box, lining up the two holes. This thick board will make it much harder for an animal—or a starling—to reach inside far enough to get to the nest.

A different way to discourage predators is to attach a metal shield around the post below the birdhouse. This can be a wide, flat metal collar, or, even better, a metal baffle that has been shaped into a cone. Point the wide end down. Mount the guard just below the box, nailing or wiring it in place high enough so an animal cannot jump over it from the ground. If you prefer, you can make a guard out of an upside-down plastic wastebasket, cutting a hole in the bottom small enough so the basket will cling to the pole just below the nesting box. Cut any rim off so animals can't use it as a foothold. Put the guard on the pole before you plant the pole in the ground.

There's not very much you can do to protect bluebirds from the cold, another enemy, except to leave your nesting box in place all year. Sometimes birds will huddle together in it during bad weather, especially at night. In some areas where bluebirds stay all year, people make special winter roosting boxes for them with enough room for quite a few chilly birds.

Sometimes people are a bird's worst enemy. Whether they are mean or just curious, people may disturb the birds so much they will fly away and never come back. That's why it's so important to mount your house in an out-of-the-way place and, if necessary, above eye level. Talk to your friends, neighbors, and family about your

41

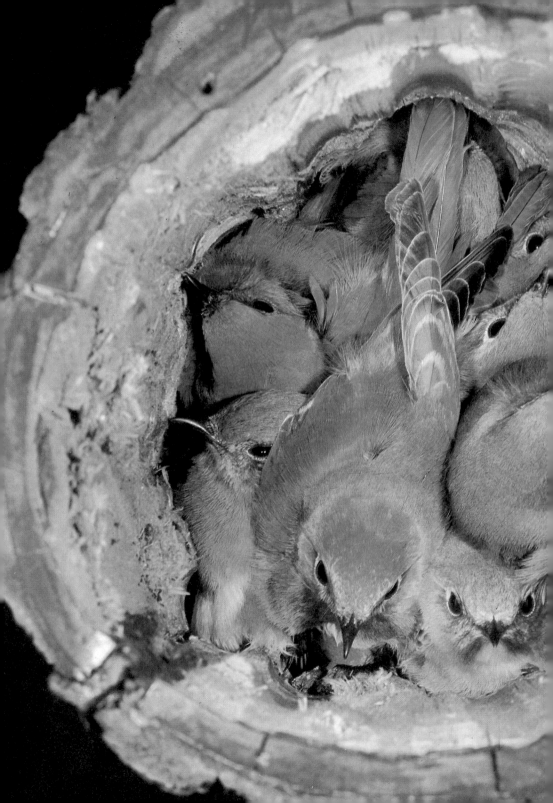

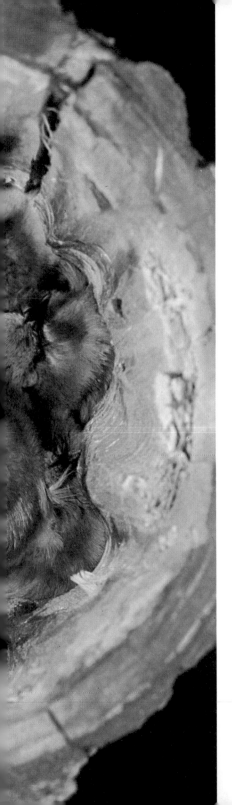

bluebird project. Explain that the birdhouse must not be disturbed.

Once young bluebirds leave the nest, they won't return, living instead in trees and bushes. To encourage their parents to raise another brood the same year, take out the old nest as soon as possible, unless they have already begun to build another nest on top of the old one. In that case, leave it alone. You may not have to wait long this time for new bluebird neighbors.

These adult male and female Eastern Bluebirds are roosting together to keep warm during the night.

Building a Bluebird Trail

If you and your friends get together, you can start a bluebird trail—the best way to attract a large number of the birds to your neighborhood. A bluebird trail is simply many bluebird houses mounted one after another in a continuous line. The houses must be at least one hundred yards apart. The line may be quite straight, perhaps along the sides of a country road. Or it may be curved or circular, maybe going around a farm, a golf course, or even a whole village. It can be short, with only a dozen birdhouses or so. Or it can be very long, going on for miles and miles, with hundreds of houses. The world's longest bluebird trail, in Canada, is about two thousand miles long! Every year, about five thousand baby bluebirds are hatched along that trail.

Many bluebird trails are organized and maintained by young people, often working with Scout or Camp Fire groups or with 4-H, garden, and bird clubs. Sometimes bluebird trails are classroom projects, with students learning about bluebirds while helping them to survive.

The reason for lining up nesting boxes in a trail is to make monitoring easier. The circular trail that starts and ends at the same place is the easiest of all. During nesting season, you can make your weekly inspection on foot, on a bicycle or a horse, or riding in a car, moving along from one nesting box to the next.

If you would like to make your own trail, here are some important tips to keep in mind:

Start out small. Don't build more houses than you will be able to monitor. You can always add others or start new trails later on.

Number the houses so you can easily keep records of the eggs laid and the babies hatched.

Attach a small weatherproof label to each birdhouse, telling your name or the name of your group along with a message like "Please do not disturb. Help save the bluebirds."

Divide the responsibility for sections of the trail among different people or groups if your trail becomes very long.

Recruit a leader. Your group leader, a parent, or a responsible young person may agree to be in charge.

Don't forget to make your trail in the right environment (open space, scattered trees, short vegetation, an area not too close to many buildings and people) and with the houses properly spaced or all your work may be wasted. And, of course, if your trail will cross public or private property, you must get permission for it before you begin.

Remember that it may take time for the bluebirds to find your houses and decide to settle down there. In the meantime, be sure some members of your group monitor the boxes from early spring through August so they will

always be clean and free of uninvited guests. All your work will be rewarded when bluebirds come home to live in your neighborhood again after an absence of so many years.

Glossary

brood   birds hatched and raised at the same time.

extinct   no longer existing.

fledgling   a young bird that has just acquired the feathers it needs to fly.

habitat   the place where an animal naturally lives or a plant naturally grows.

incubate   to keep eggs at a certain temperature so they will hatch; birds incubate their eggs by sitting on them.

instinct   behavior that occurs naturally, that does not have to be learned.

migrate   to move periodically from one area to another for food and breeding.

molt   to shed feathers.

nestling   a young bird that has not yet left the nest.

predator   an animal that preys upon another.

species   a group of animals or plants that are similar to one another and reproduce only among themselves; there are three species of bluebirds: Eastern, Western, and Mountain.

thrush   the family of birds to which all three species of bluebirds belong.